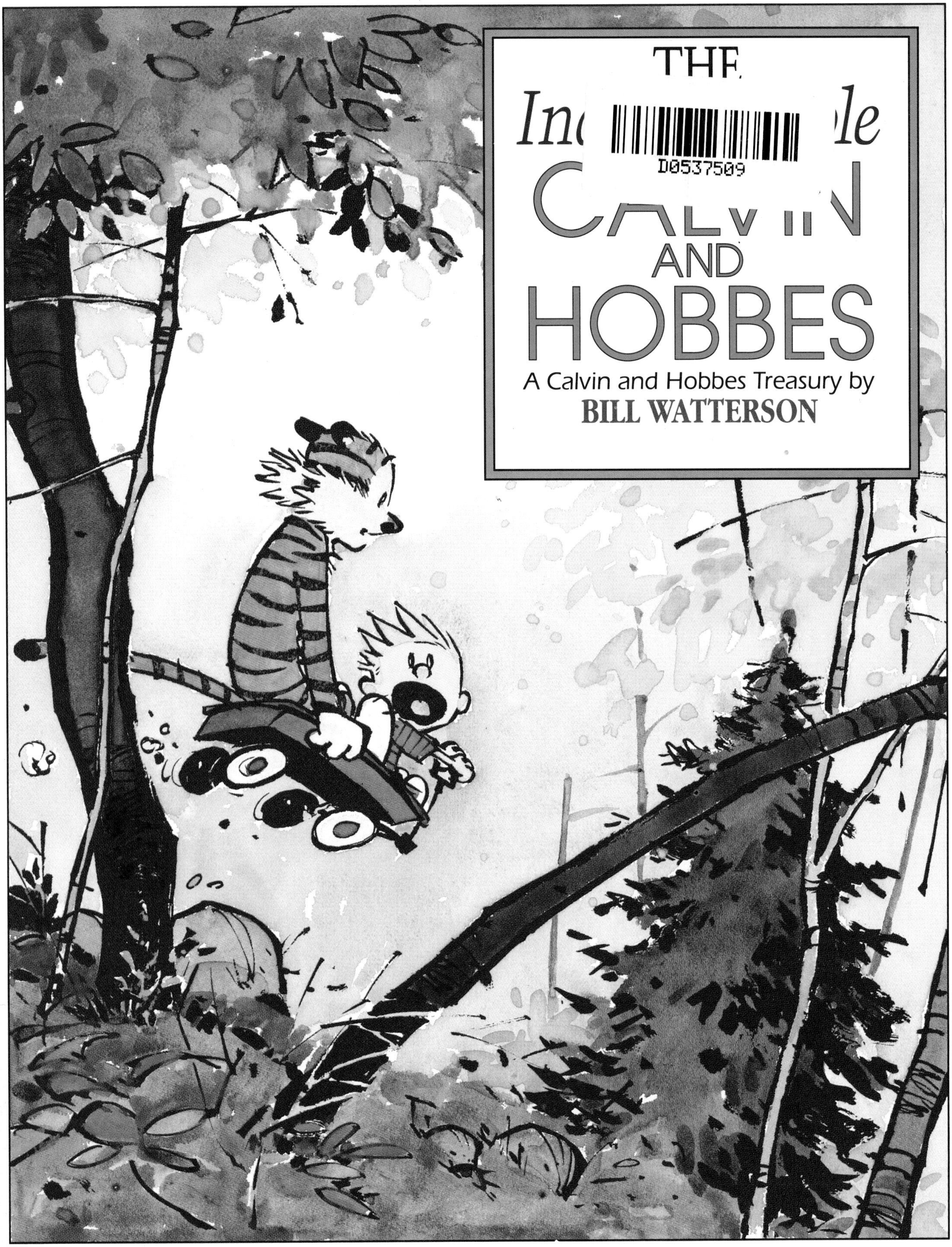

THE Ind[illegible]le CALVIN AND HOBBES

A Calvin and Hobbes Treasury by

BILL WATTERSON

WARNER BOOKS

A *Warner* Book

First published in Great Britain in 1992 by Warner Books
First published in the USA by Andrews and McMeel 1992
Reprinted 1994

Copyright © 1992 by Bill Watterson, distributed
by Universal Press Syndicate

Includes cartoons from *The Revenge of the Baby-Sat* and
Scientific Progress Goes 'Boink'

The moral right of the author has been asserted.

A CIP catalogue record for this book
is available from the British Library

ISBN 0 7515 0028 3

Printed and bound in Great Britain by
The Bath Press

Warner Books
A Division of
Little, Brown and Company (UK)
Brettenham House
Lancaster Place
London WC2E 7EN

I made a big decision a little while ago.
I don't remember what it was, which prob'ly goes to show
That many times a simple choice can prove to be essential
Even though it often might appear inconsequential.

I must have been distracted when I left my home because
Left or right I'm sure I went. (I wonder which it was!)
Anyway, I never veered: I walked in that direction
Utterly absorbed, it seems, in quiet introspection.

For no reason I can think of, I've wandered far astray.
And that is how I got to where I find myself today.

Explorers are we, intrepid and bold,
Out in the wild, amongst wonders untold.
Equipped with our wits, a map, and a snack,
We're searching for fun and we're on the right track!

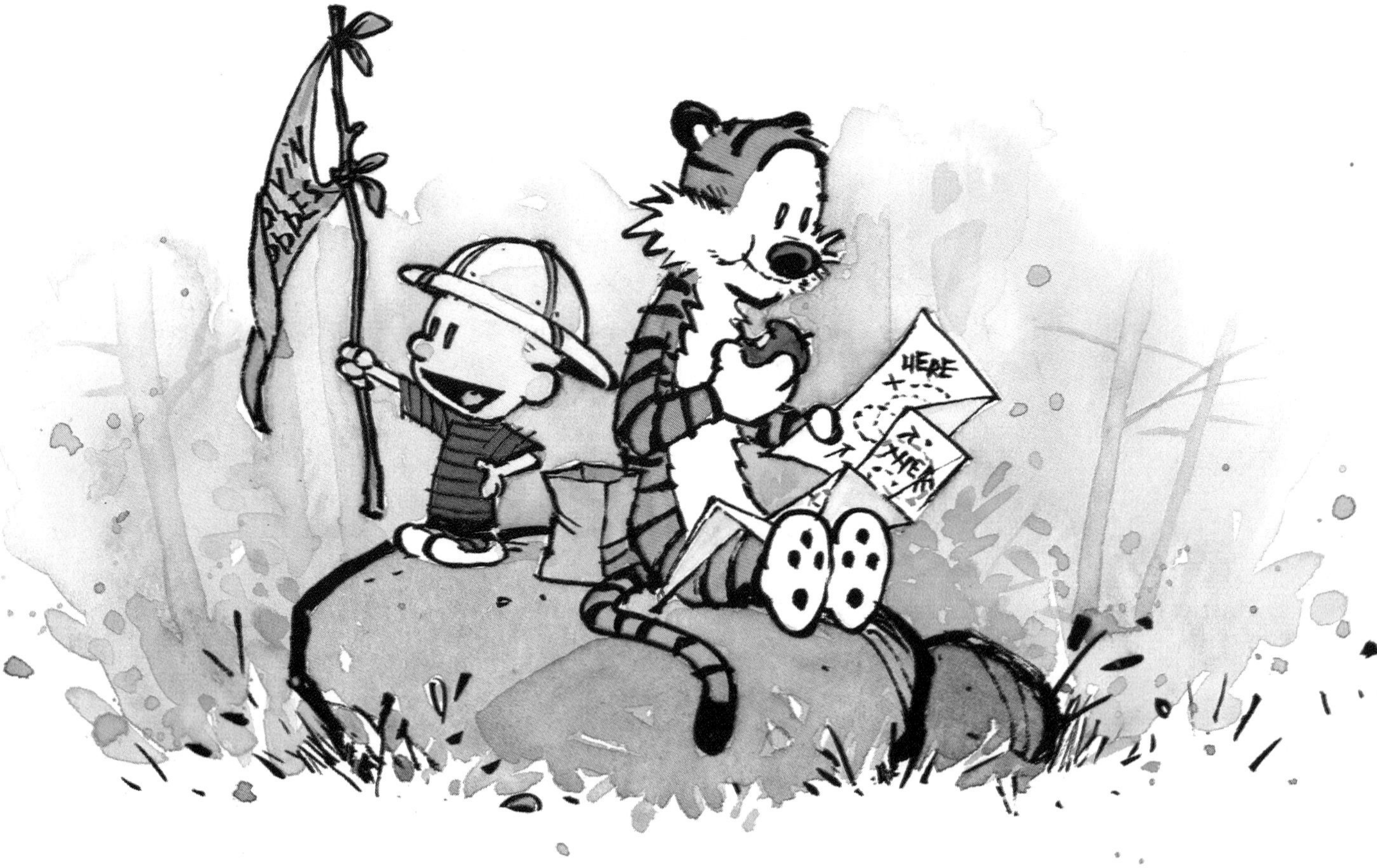
HERE

My mother has eyes on the back of her head!
I don't quite believe it, but that's what she said.
She explained that she'd been so uniquely endowed
To catch me when I did Things Not Allowed.
I think she must also have eyes on her rear.
I've noticed her hindsight is unusually clear.

At night my mind does not much care
If what it thinks is here or there.
It tells me stories it invents
And makes up things that don't make sense.
I don't know why it does this stuff.
The real world seems quite weird enough.

What if my bones were in a museum,
Where aliens paid good money to see 'em?
And suppose that they'd put me together all wrong,
Sticking bones on to bones where they didn't belong!

Imagine phalanges, pelvis, and spine
Welded to mandibles that once had been mine!
With each misassemblage, the error compounded,
The aliens would draw back in terror, astounded!

Their textbooks would show me in grim illustration,
The most hideous thing ever seen in creation!
The museum would commission a model in plaster
Of ME, to be called, "Evolution's Disaster"!

And paleontologists there would debate
Dozens of theories to help postulate
How man survived for those thousands of years
With teeth-covered arms growing out of his ears!

Oh, I hope that I'm never in such manner displayed,
No matter HOW much to see me the aliens paid.

I did not want to go with them.
Alas, I had no choice.
This was made quite clear to me
In threat'ning tones of voice.

I protested mightily
And scrambled 'cross the floor.
But though I grabbed the furniture,
They dragged me out the door.

In the car, I screamed and moaned.
I cried my red eyes dry.
The window down, I yelled for help
To people we passed by.

Mom and Dad can make the rules
And certain things forbid,
But I can make them wish that they
Had never had a kid.

Now I'm in bed,
The sheets pulled to my head.
My tiger is here making Zs.
He's furry and hot.
He takes up a lot
Of the bed and he's hogging the breeze.

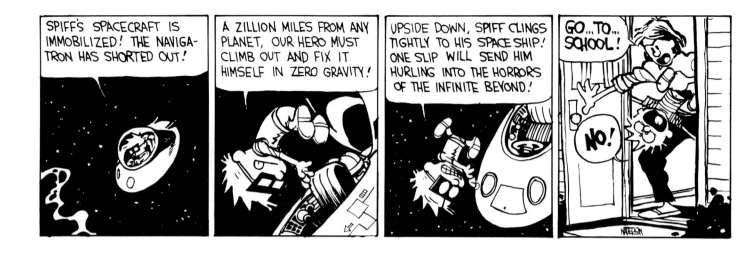

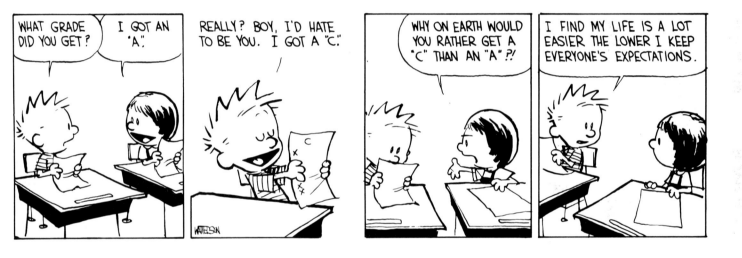

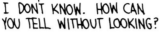

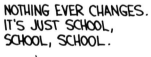

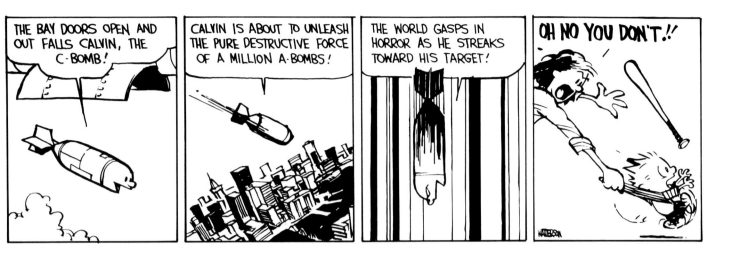

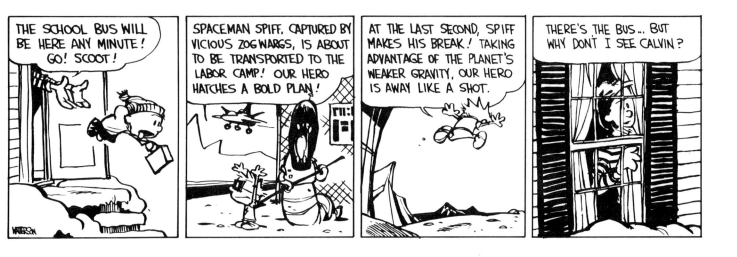

31

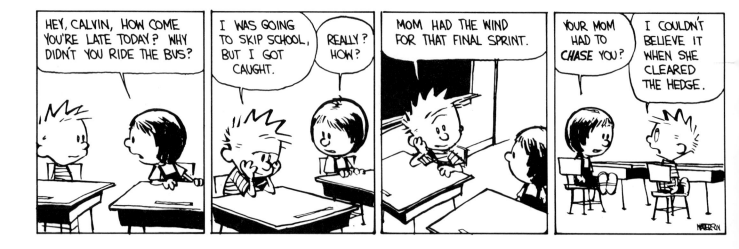

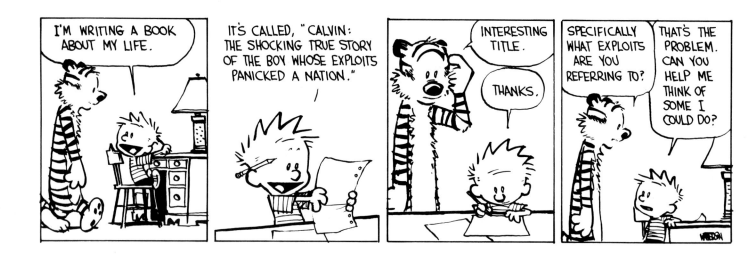

43

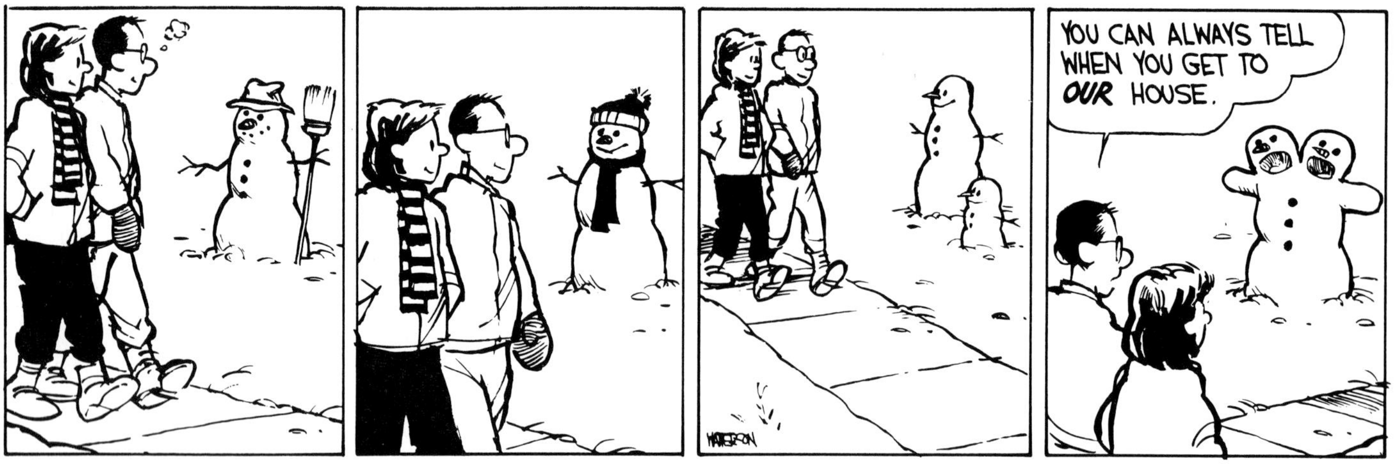
YOU CAN ALWAYS TELL WHEN YOU GET TO **OUR** HOUSE.

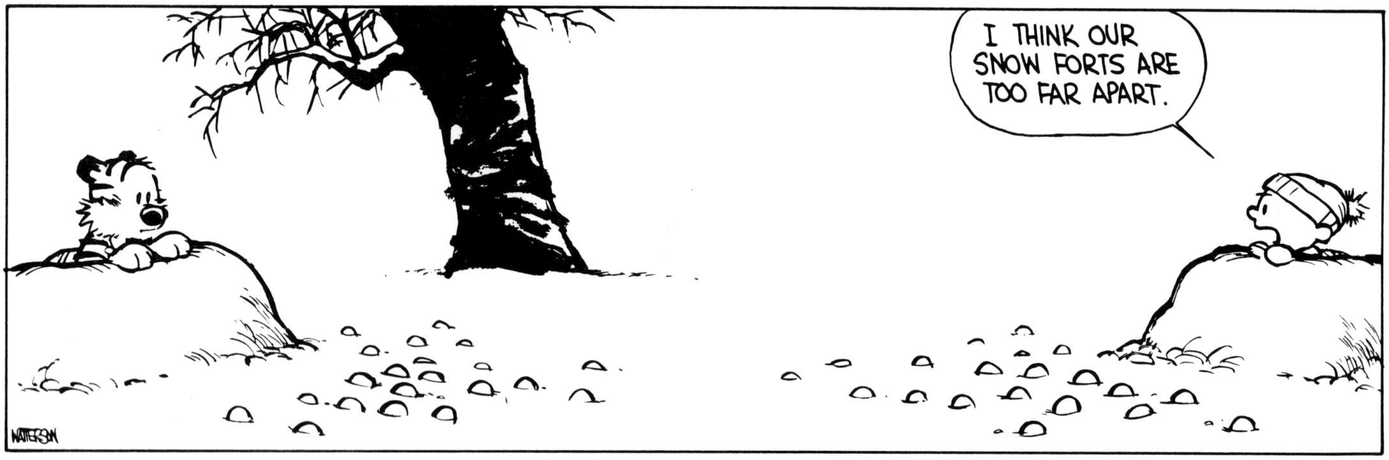
I THINK OUR SNOW FORTS ARE TOO FAR APART.

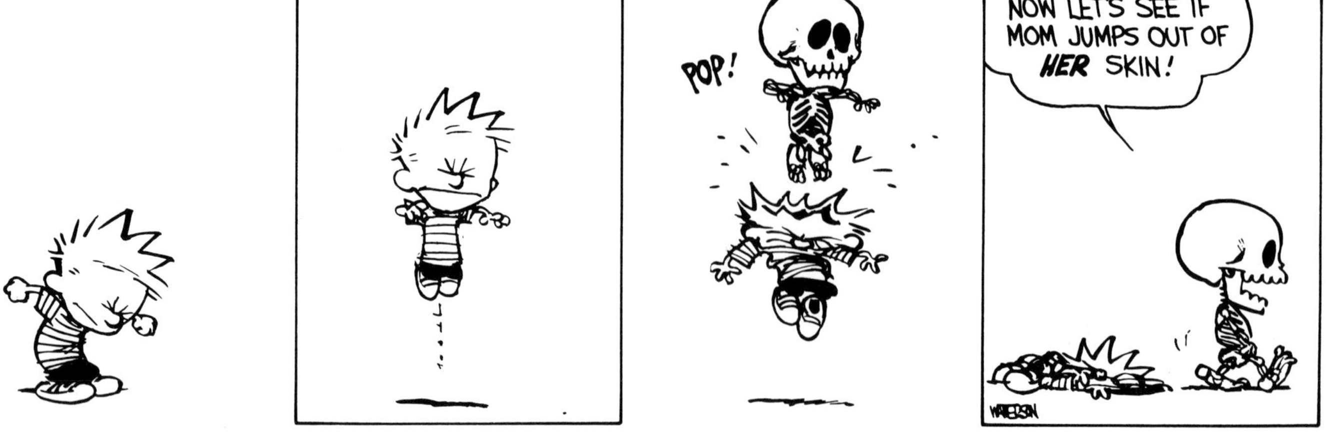
NOW LET'S SEE IF MOM JUMPS OUT OF **HER** SKIN!

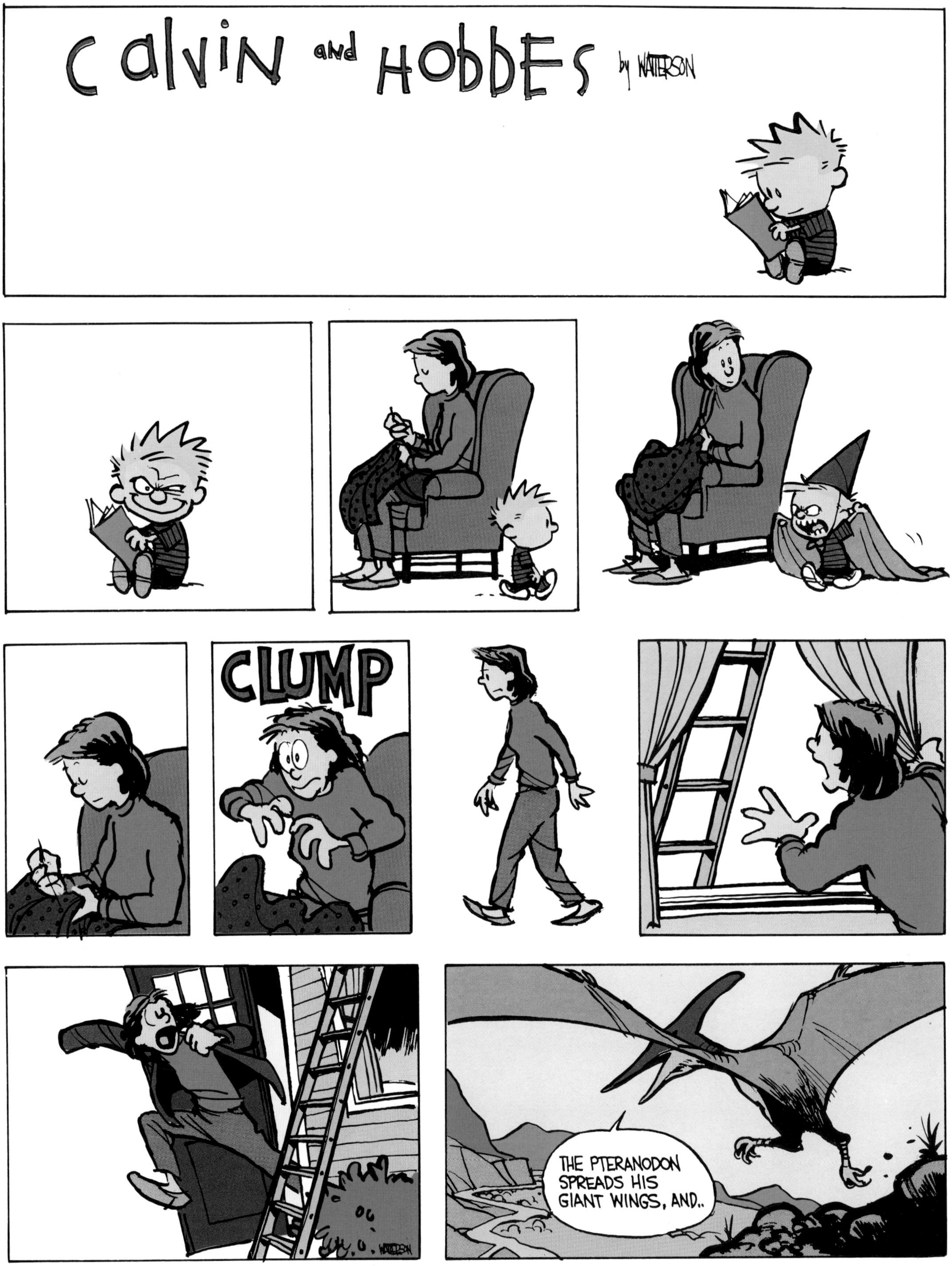
Calvin and HOBBES by WATTERSON
CLUMP
THE PTERANODON SPREADS HIS GIANT WINGS, AND..
WATTERSON

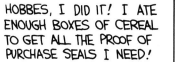

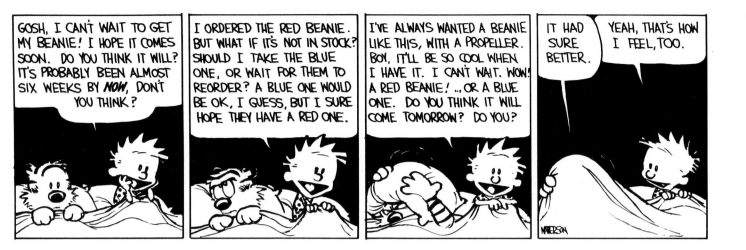

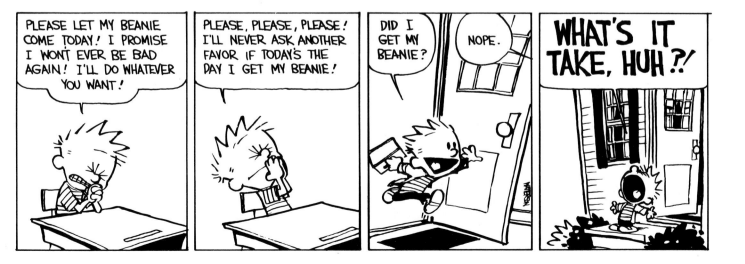

52

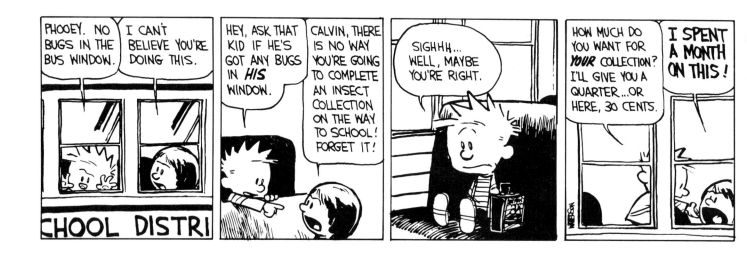

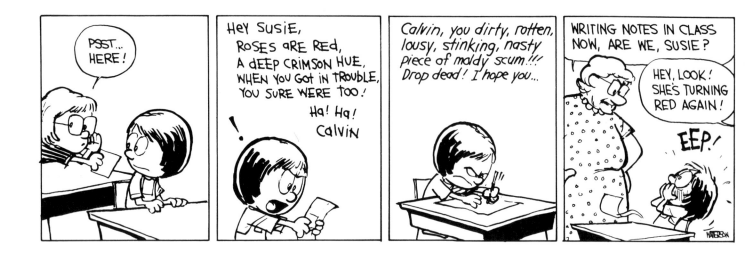

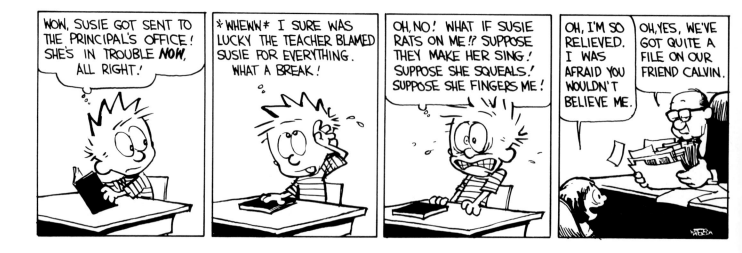

61

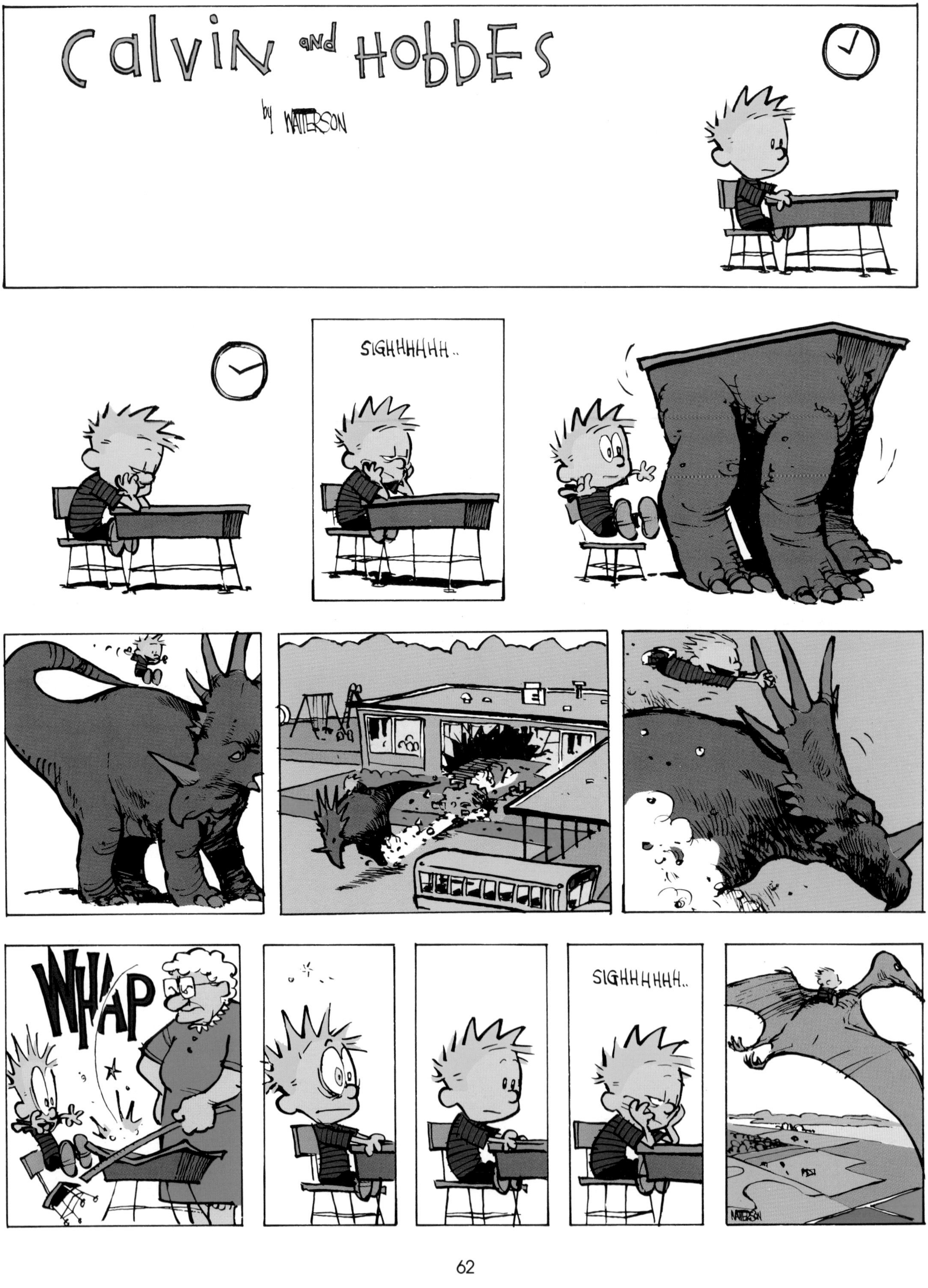
Calvin and Hobbes
by WATTERSON
SIGHHHHHH..
WHAP
SIGHHHHHH..
WATTERSON

HOW COME **YOU** ALWAYS READ ME MY BEDTIME STORY AND NOT MOM?

BECAUSE READING THE BEDTIME STORY IS THE **DAD'S** JOB.

AND IT APPEARS TO BE THE **ONLY** "DAD'S JOB" AROUND HERE!

LEFT THE DISHES FOR MOM AGAIN, HUH?

TONIGHT'S STORY IS CALLED, "WHY PRINCE CHARMING STAYED SINGLE."

PRINCE **WHAT**?

I'VE BEEN THINKING. SUPPOSE I GROW UP TO BE ONE OF THE WORLD'S GREATEST MEN OF ALL TIME. SUPPOSE MY NAME WILL BE AN INSPIRATION TO HUMANITY FOR EONS TO COME!

WHAT WILL THE HISTORY BOOKS SAY? THEY'LL SAY, "MUCH OF HIS CHILDHOOD WAS SPENT UNWILLINGLY IN THE BATHTUB."

WHAT AN INDIGNITY THIS BATH IS! IS THIS SITUATION WORTHY OF ONE OF THE GREATEST MEN OF ALL TIME?!?

MY LIKELY HISTORICAL SIGNIFICANCE IS A TERRIBLE BURDEN.

WOULD YOU RATHER THEY SAID YOUR CHILDHOOD WAS DIRTY AND SMELLY?

NNNGKGKK

HOCCHHHH

PTOOEY!

BOY, THEY SURE GO FARTHER WHEN YOU MAKE 'EM RIGHT!

LET'S MAKE UP A **NEW** CONTEST, OK?

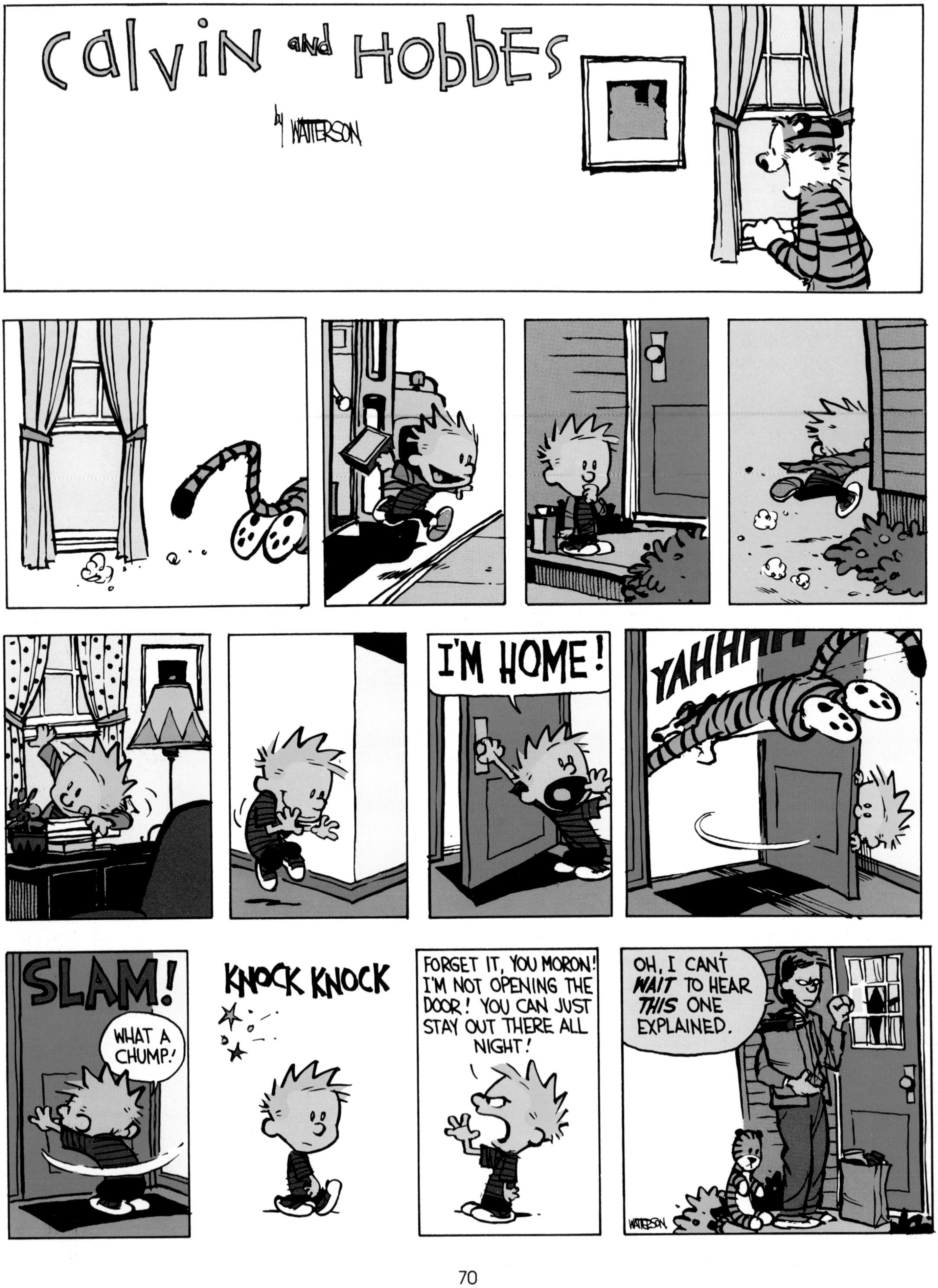
Calvin and Hobbes
by WATTERSON
I'M HOME!
YAHHHH
SLAM!
WHAT A CHUMP!
KNOCK KNOCK
FORGET IT, YOU MORON! I'M NOT OPENING THE DOOR! YOU CAN JUST STAY OUT THERE ALL NIGHT!
OH, I CAN'T WAIT TO HEAR THIS ONE EXPLAINED.
WATTERSON

IS CALVIN ASLEEP?

YES, HE'S SNUGGLED UP WITH HOBBES.

BOY, I DON'T KNOW HOW *I'M* EVER GOING TO SLEEP.

ME NEITHER. I CAN'T GET OVER WHAT'S HAPPENED.

THE IDEA OF SOME CRAZY STRANGER GOING THROUGH OUR HOUSE... *BRRRR!!* I WISH *I* HAD A BIG STUFFED ANIMAL TO FEEL SAFE WITH.

I GUESS YOU'LL HAVE TO DO.

SO WHAT DO *I* GET TO SNUGGLE? HOW COME *I'M* THE GROWN-UP??

THIS IS GOING TO BE A LONG NIGHT.

MY HEART JUMPS AT THE SLIGHTEST SOUND. IT'S ALMOST 2, AND I'M WIDE AWAKE.

WHEN SOMEONE BREAKS INTO YOUR HOME, IT SHATTERS YOUR LAST ILLUSION OF SECURITY. IF YOU'RE NOT SAFE IN YOUR OWN HOME, YOU'RE NOT SAFE ANYWHERE.

A MAN'S HOME IS HIS CASTLE, BUT IT SHOULDN'T HAVE TO BE A FORTRESS.

ARE YOU STILL AWAKE TOO?

MM-HMM. I WAS THINKING.

IT'S FUNNY... WHEN I WAS A KID, I THOUGHT GROWN-UPS NEVER WORRIED ABOUT ANYTHING. I TRUSTED MY PARENTS TO TAKE CARE OF EVERYTHING, AND IT NEVER OCCURRED TO ME THAT THEY MIGHT NOT KNOW HOW.

I FIGURED THAT ONCE YOU GREW UP, YOU AUTOMATICALLY KNEW WHAT TO DO IN ANY GIVEN SCENARIO.

I DON'T THINK I'D HAVE BEEN IN SUCH A HURRY TO REACH ADULTHOOD IF I'D KNOWN THE WHOLE THING WAS GOING TO BE AD-LIBBED.

WELL, AT LEAST WE WEREN'T HOME WHEN OUR HOUSE WAS BROKEN INTO. NO ONE WAS HURT. WE'RE ALL TOGETHER AND OK.

WE LOST A FEW OF OUR NICE THINGS, BUT THINGS DON'T MATTER MUCH REALLY.

IT'S HARD TO BELIEVE HOW OFTEN WE FORGET THAT.

CAN I BE EXCUSED NOW?

YOU DIDN'T FINISH YOUR DINNER.

WELL, I DIDN'T LIKE IT VERY MUCH, AND THERE'S THIS TV SHOW I WANT TO WATCH, SO...

OUR TV WAS STOLEN, REMEMBER?

GOSH, I GUESS I'LL EAT MY ASPARAGUS, DO MY HOMEWORK, AND GO STRAIGHT TO BED, THEN.

AND WE'RE SO PROUD OF HOW YOU HANDLE ADVERSITY.

THIS IS WHERE OUR TELEVISION USED TO BE.

BUT WE DON'T HAVE A TV ANYMORE. NOW WE HAVE A BLANK WALL TO WATCH.

SO HERE I AM, NOT BEING ENTERTAINED.

A POINTLESS EXISTENCE, HUH?

I MEAN, THE WALL IS EVEN PLAIN OLD *WHITE!*

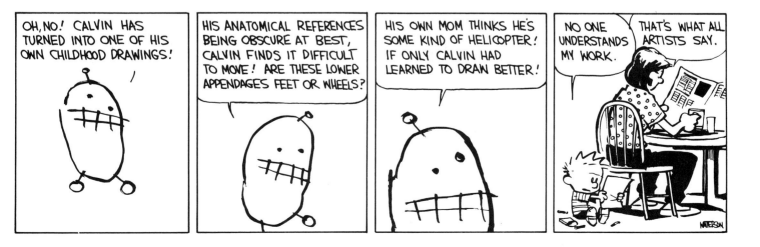

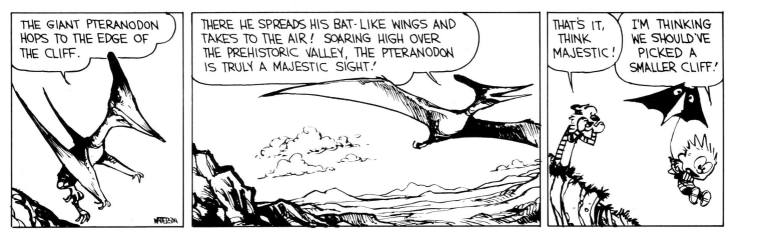

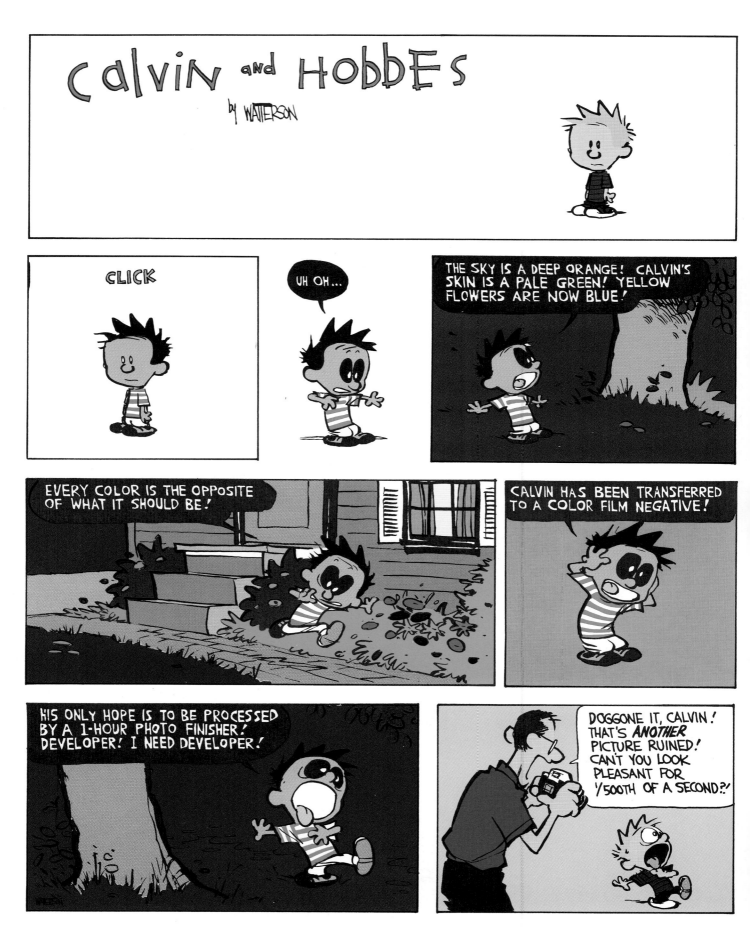

CALVIN AND HOBBES by WATTERSON

I PERFORMED A SCIENTIFIC EXPERIMENT TODAY.

YOU KNOW HOW MAPS ALWAYS SHOW NORTH AS UP AND SOUTH AS DOWN? I WANTED TO SEE IF THAT WAS TRUE OR NOT.

WHAT DID YOU FIND OUT?

NOT MUCH. YOUR COMPASS DIDN'T SURVIVE THE TRIP SOUTH FROM THE TOP OF THE TREE.

MY COMPASS?!

LET ME KNOW WHEN YOU GET A NEW ONE. MY JUNIOR SCIENTIST BOOK SAYS NOT TO GET DISCOURAGED BY TEMPORARY SETBACKS.

I'VE BEEN THINKING. YOU KNOW HOW BORING DAD IS? MAYBE IT'S A BIG PHONY ACT!

MAYBE AFTER HE PUTS US TO BED, DAD DONS SOME WEIRD COSTUME AND GOES OUT FIGHTING CRIME! MAYBE THIS WHOLE "DAD" STUFF IS JUST A SECRET IDENTITY!

MAYBE THE MAYOR CALLS DAD ON A SECRET HOT LINE WHENEVER THE CITY'S IN TROUBLE! MAYBE DAD'S A MASKED SUPERHERO!

IF THAT'S TRUE HE SHOULD DRIVE A COOLER CAR.

I KNOW. OURS DOESN'T EVEN HAVE A CASSETTE DECK.

THERE'S THE STEGOSAURUS OUT FRONT! THERE'S THE NATURAL HISTORY MUSEUM! HOORAY!

I CAN'T WAIT TO SEE ALL THE DINOSAURS! C'MON, LET'S HURRY!

IT'S CERTAINLY BEEN A WHILE SINCE WE'VE BEEN HERE, HASN'T IT?

AT THE MUSEUM'S REQUEST, YES.

OH, THAT'S RIGHT, CALVIN, NO BITING PEOPLE THIS TIME, REMEMBER?

RROWRR

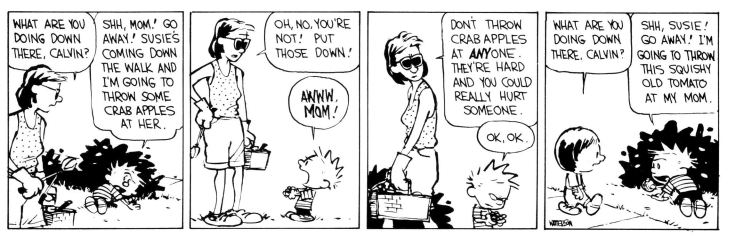

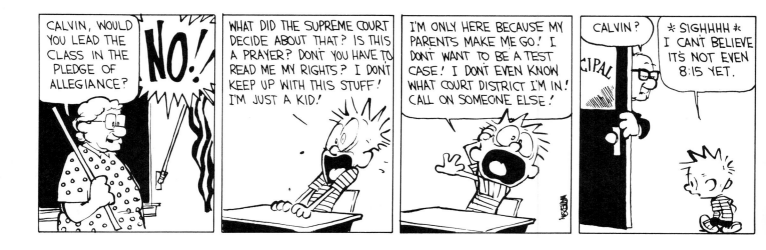

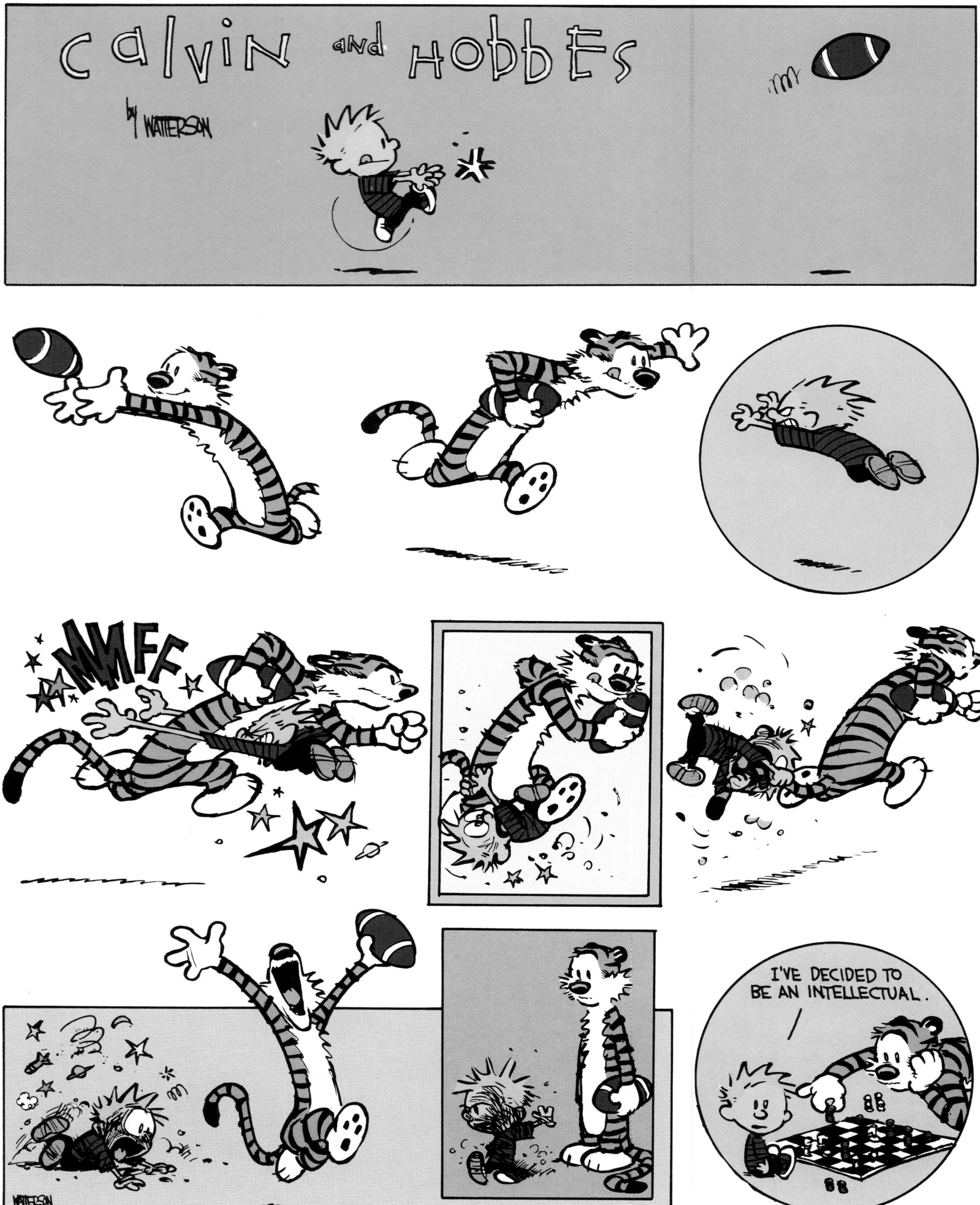
Calvin and HOBBES
by WATTERSON
MMFF
I'VE DECIDED TO BE AN INTELLECTUAL.
WATTERSON

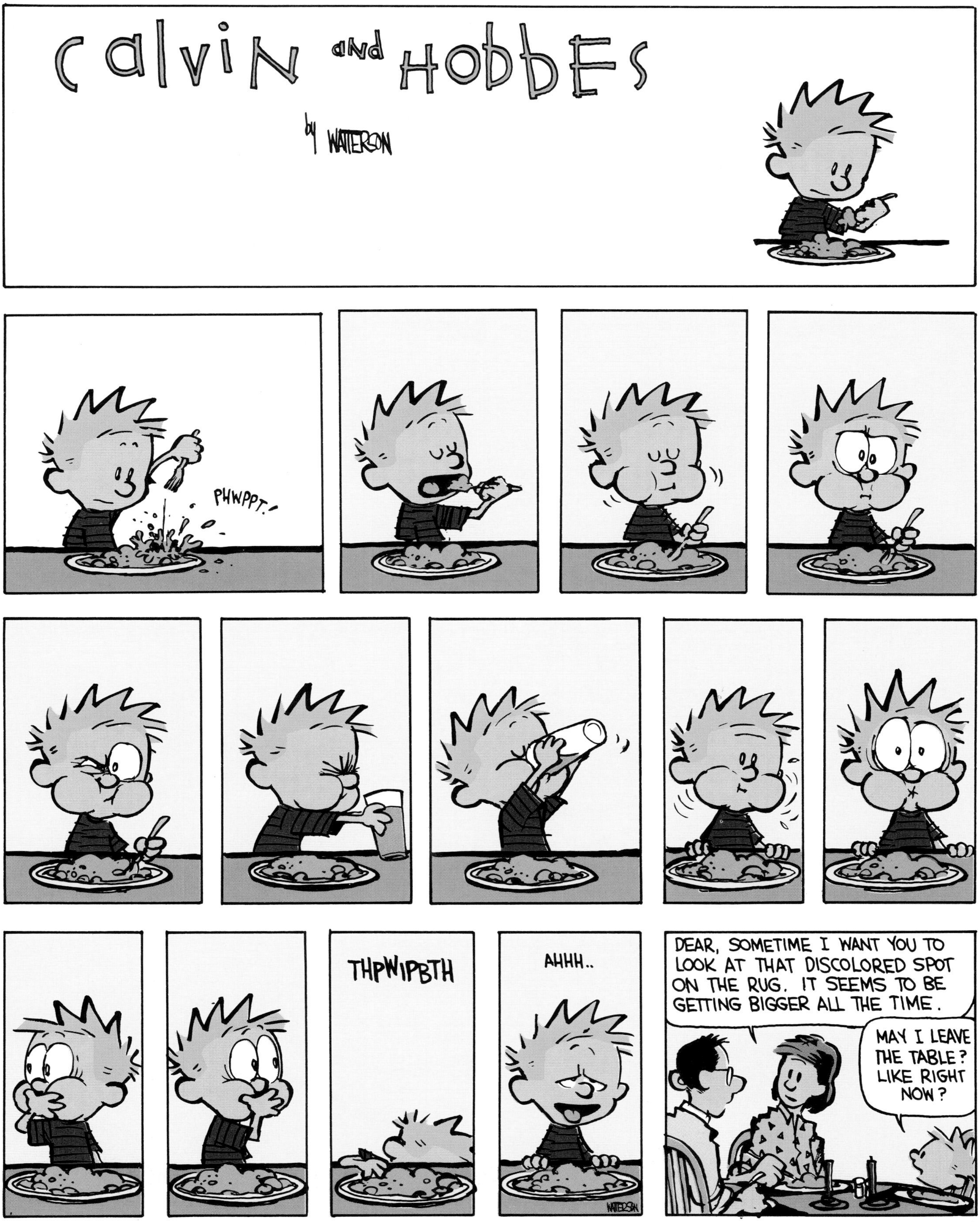
Calvin and Hobbes
by WATTERSON
PHWPPT!
THPWIPBTH
AHHH..
DEAR, SOMETIME I WANT YOU TO LOOK AT THAT DISCOLORED SPOT ON THE RUG. IT SEEMS TO BE GETTING BIGGER ALL THE TIME.
MAY I LEAVE THE TABLE? LIKE RIGHT NOW?
WATTERSON

BY GOLLY, I *AM* GOING TO STEAL MY TRUCK BACK FROM MOE! IT'S MINE AND HE HAS NO RIGHT TO HAVE IT!

I'LL JUST SNEAK UP BEHIND THE SWINGS HERE, AND WHEN MOE'S NOT LOOKING, I'LL RUN UP, GRAB THE TRUCK AND TAKE OFF!

THIS PLAYGROUND SHOULD HAVE ONE OF THOSE AUTOMATIC INSURANCE MACHINES LIKE THEY HAVE IN AIRPORTS.

OK, MOE'S GOT HIS BACK TO ME! NOW I'LL ZIP OVER, STEAL MY TRUCK BACK AND RUN LIKE CRAZY!

HE'LL NEVER KNOW WHAT HIT HIM! BY THE TIME HE SEES THE TRUCK IS GONE, I'LL BE A MILE AWAY! IT'S A FAIL-PROOF PLAN! NOTHING CAN GO WRONG! IT'S A SNAP!

THERE'S NO REASON TO HESITATE. IT'LL BE OVER IN A SPLIT SECOND, AND I'LL SURE BE GLAD TO HAVE MY TRUCK BACK! I'LL JUST DO IT AND BE DONE! NOTHING TO IT! IT'S EASY!

OBVIOUSLY MY BODY DOESN'T BELIEVE A WORD MY BRAIN IS SAYING.

PHOOEY, WHO AM I KIDDING? I'D NEVER GET AWAY WITH STEALING MY TRUCK BACK FROM MOE. THE UGLY GALOOT IS THE SIZE OF A BUICK.

HMM... SINCE I CAN'T *FIGHT* HIM, MAYBE I SHOULD TRY *TALKING* TO HIM. MAYBE IF I REASONED WITH HIM, HE'D SEE *MY* SIDE.

MAYBE HE'D REALIZE THAT STEALING HURTS PEOPLE, AND MAYBE HE'D RETURN MY TRUCK *WILLINGLY*.

MAYBE IF I'M REALLY LUCKY I WON'T GO THROUGH LIFE WITH THE NICKNAME "OMELET FACE."

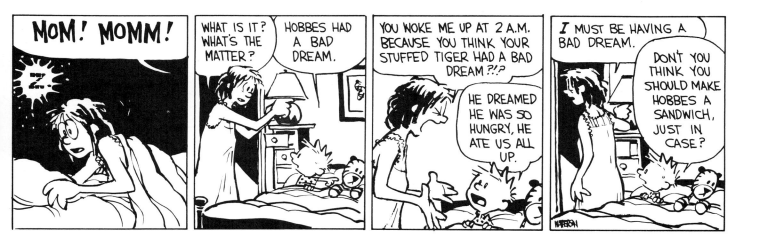

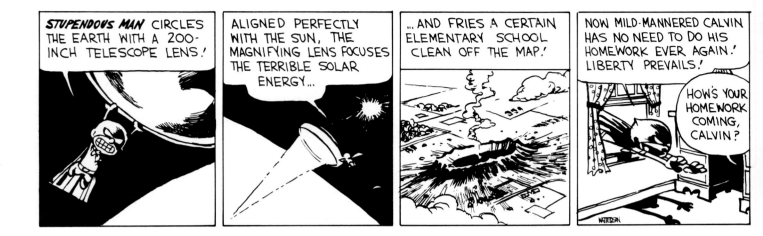

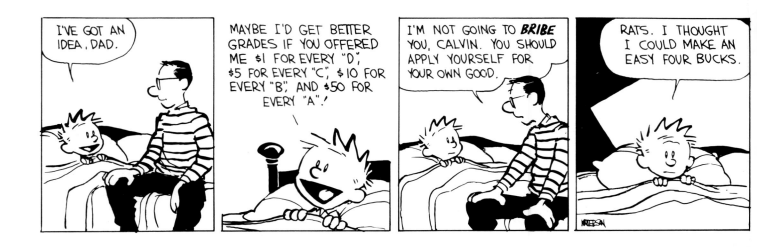

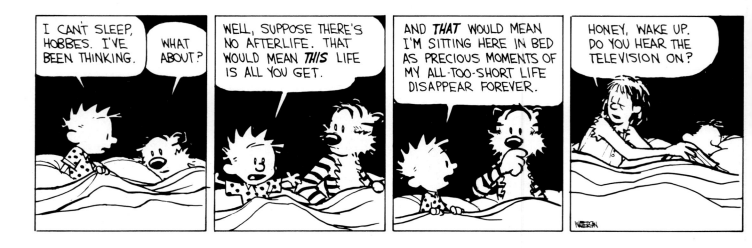

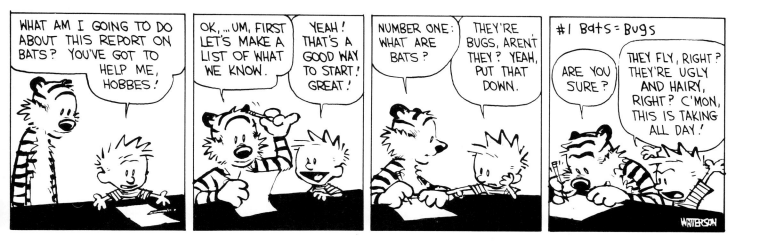

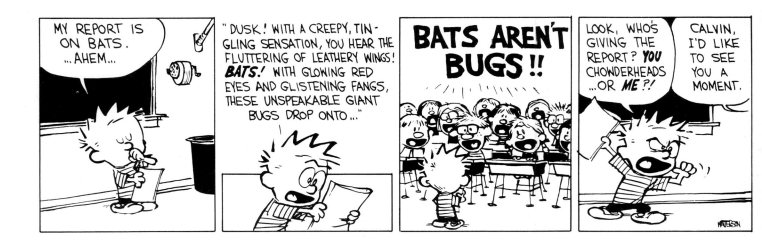

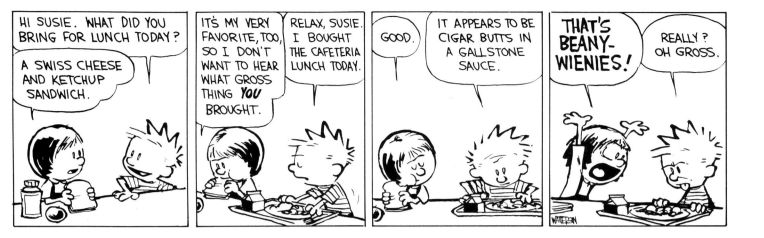

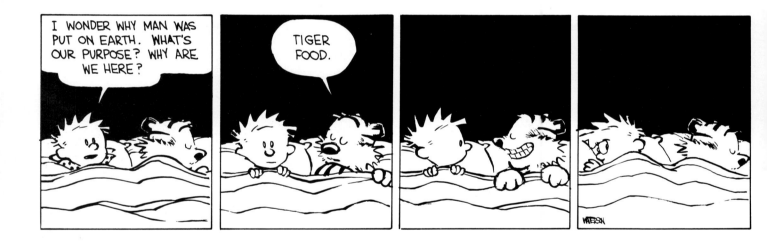

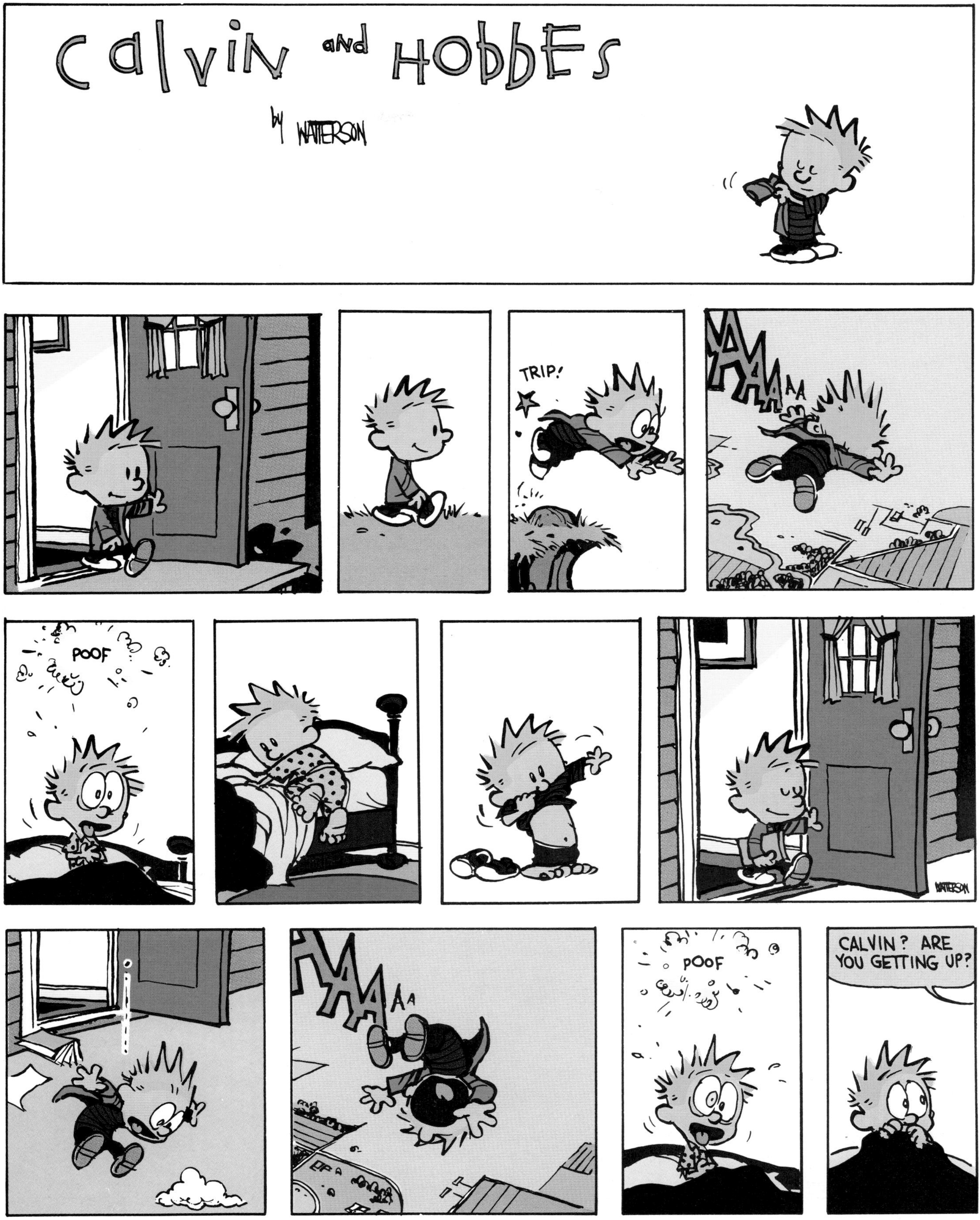
Calvin and HOBBES
by WATTERSON
TRIP!
AAAAAAA
POOF
WATTERSON
AAAAA
POOF
CALVIN? ARE YOU GETTING UP?

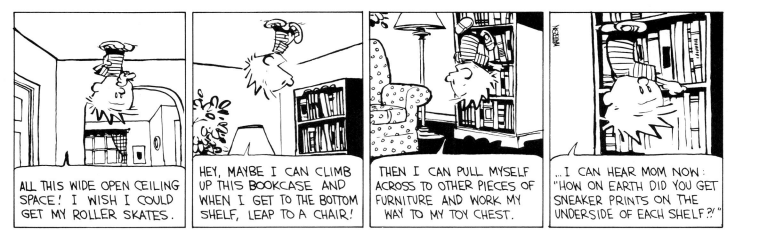

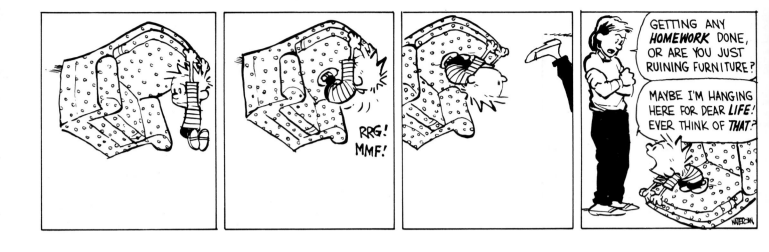

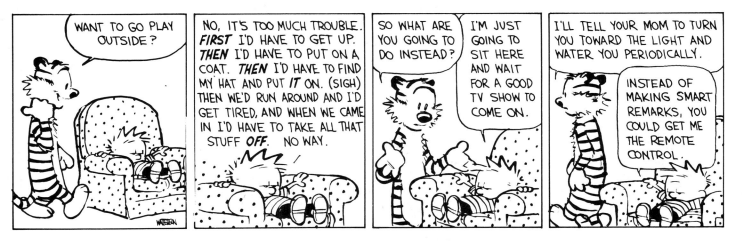

THIS IS THE PART OF WINTER I LIKE BEST... WHEN YOU COME INSIDE, FREEZING COLD AND SOAKED...

...AND YOU PUT ON FRESH DRY CLOTHES, AND RUN UP TO THE WARM KITCHEN, WHERE MOM'S GOT A STEAMING MUG OF HOT CHOCOLATE WAITING FOR YOU!

MOM?... MOM??
HEY MOM!

"CALVIN, I'M NEXT DOOR. DON'T HAVE ANYTHING TO EAT, OR YOU'LL SPOIL YOUR APPETITE. MOM."

IT'S GOING TO BE A LONG, COLD, DARK WINTER.

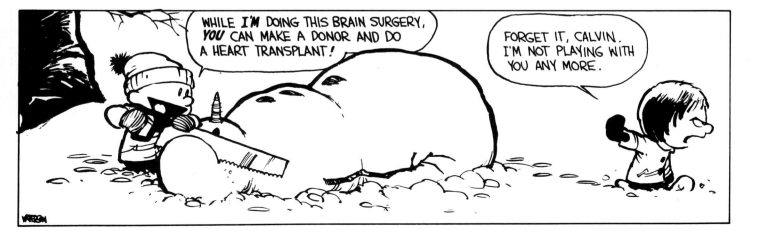

WHILE I'M DOING THIS BRAIN SURGERY, YOU CAN MAKE A DONOR AND DO A HEART TRANSPLANT!

FORGET IT, CALVIN. I'M NOT PLAYING WITH YOU ANY MORE.

OK DUPLICATES, LISTEN UP. AS LONG AS YOU'RE ALL HERE AND I DON'T KNOW HOW TO GET RID OF YOU, WE MIGHT AS WELL COOPERATE.

SPECIFICALLY, WITH FIVE DUPLICATES, WE CAN DIVIDE UP THE SCHOOL WEEK SO THERE'S ONE DUPLICATE FOR EACH DAY.

IF THE REST OF US LAY LOW, WE CAN TAKE TURNS GOING TO SCHOOL, AND NO ONE WILL BE THE WISER!

GREAT!

NOW THAT STILL LEAVES US WITH THE QUESTION OF WHO GETS THE BED TONIGHT.

WE'LL FIGHT YOU FOR IT.

HI CALVIN.

I'M NOT CALVIN. I'M DUPLICATE NUMBER TWO.

WHAT ARE YOU TALKING ABOUT?

WE DREW STRAWS, AND TODAY'S MY DAY TO GO TO SCHOOL. WE'RE ALL TAKING TURNS SO WE EACH ONLY GO ONCE A WEEK.

CALVIN, YOU ARE SO WEIRD I'M NOT EVEN GOING TO TALK TO YOU.

I'M NOT CALVIN.

I WISH I LIVED SOMEPLACE WHERE I WENT TO A NORMAL BUS STOP.

ARE YOU IN CALVIN'S CLASS? WILL YOU HELP ME FIND HIS LOCKER?

CALVIN, WOULD YOU PLEASE DEMONSTRATE THE HOMEWORK PROBLEM YOU WERE ASSIGNED YESTERDAY?

I WASN'T HERE YESTERDAY.

YES, YOU WERE, CALVIN. DIDN'T YOU DO YOUR PROBLEM?

I'M NOT CALVIN. I'M DUPLICATE NUMBER FIVE. DUPLICATE *TWO* WAS HERE YESTERDAY, NOT *ME*. WE'RE ALL TAKING TURNS. NUMBER TWO WILL BE BACK NEXT WEEK, AND YOU CAN ASK HIM TO DO THE PROBLEM *THEN*.

LOOK, I DON'T SEE WHAT'S SO HARD ABOUT THIS!

PRINCIPAL

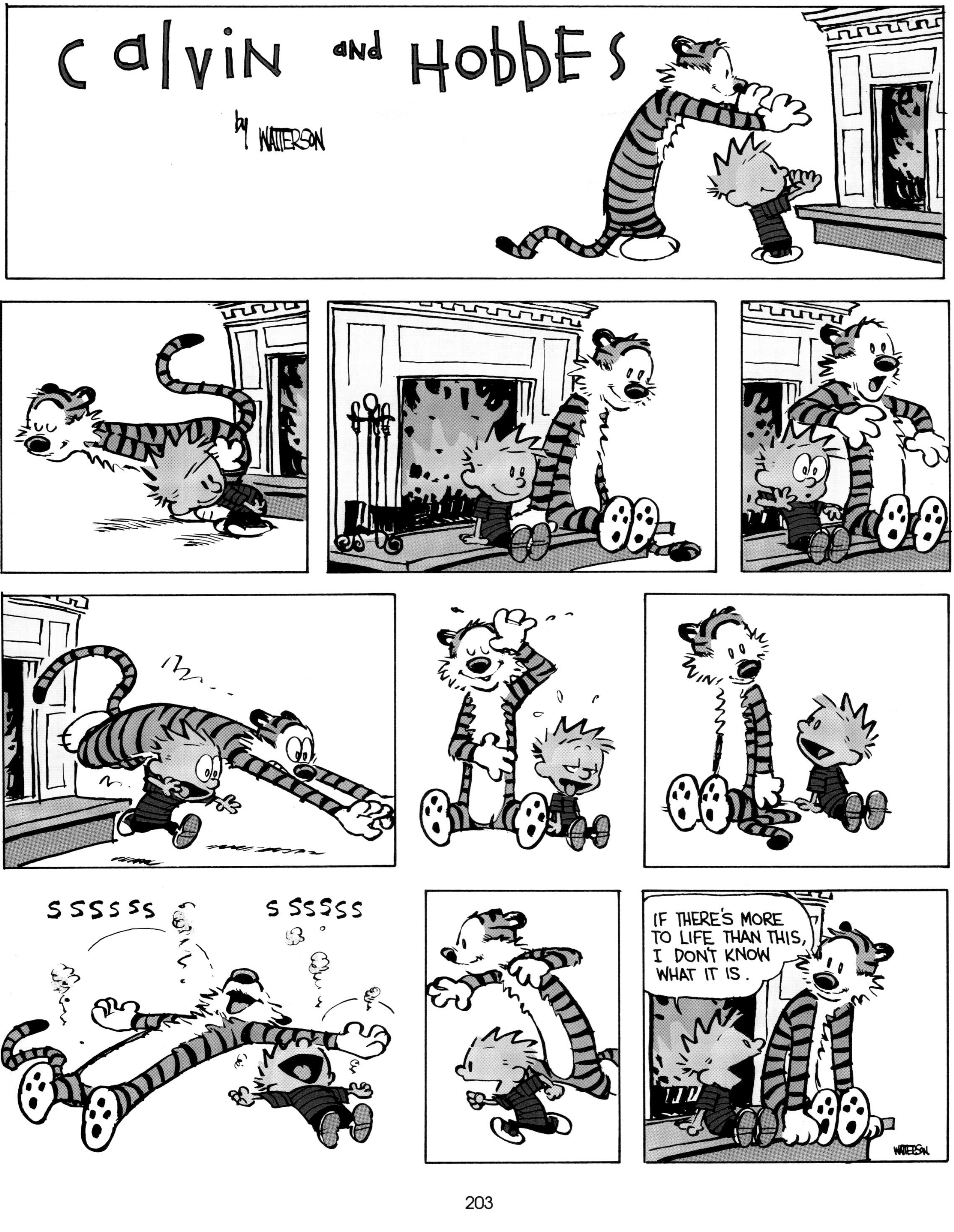
Calvin and Hobbes
by WATTERSON
SSSSSS
SSSSSS
IF THERE'S MORE TO LIFE THAN THIS, I DON'T KNOW WHAT IT IS.
WATTERSON

WHY SHOULD I GO TO SCHOOL?! WHY CAN'T I STAY HOME?

WHY DO I HAVE TO LEARN? WHY CAN'T I STAY THE WAY I AM? WHAT'S THE POINT OF THIS? WHY DO THINGS HAVE TO BE THIS WAY? WHY CAN'T THINGS BE DIFFERENT?

LIFE IS FULL OF MYSTERIES, ISN'T IT? SEE YOU THIS AFTERNOON.

AT 7:00 AM, MOM'S NOT VERY PHILOSOPHICAL.

ALL SET?

YEP!

OK, GET READY!

NOW!

CLICK

SMASH

TOO BAD THE BACK OF THE CAMERA OPENED WHEN WE LANDED. THAT WOULD'VE BEEN A GREAT PICTURE!

HA! I'VE GOT A GREAT WORD AND IT'S ON A "DOUBLE WORD SCORE" BOX!

"ZQFMGB" ISN'T A WORD! IT DOESN'T EVEN HAVE A VOWEL!

IT IS SO A WORD! IT'S A WORM FOUND IN NEW GUINEA! EVERYONE KNOWS THAT!

I'M LOOKING IT UP.

YOU DO, AND I'LL LOOK UP THAT 12-LETTER WORD YOU PLAYED WITH ALL THE Xs AND Js!

WHAT'S YOUR SCORE FOR ZQFMGB?

957.

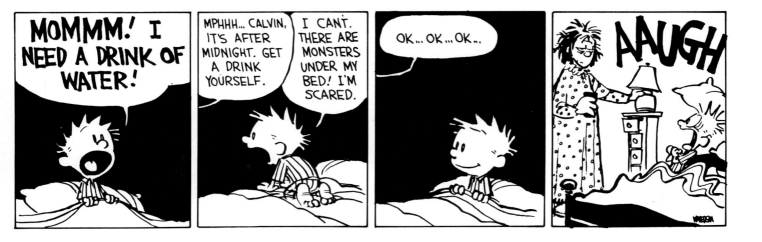

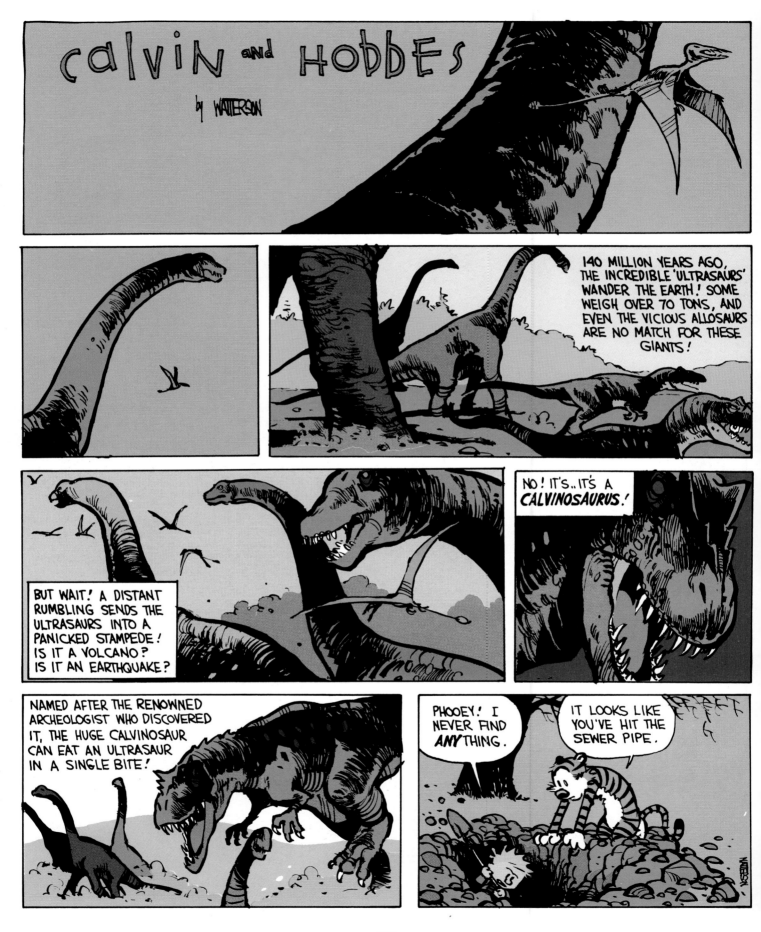

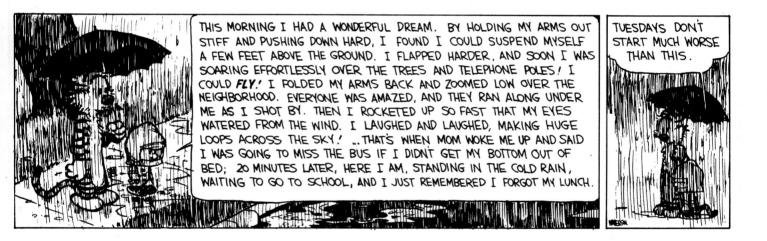

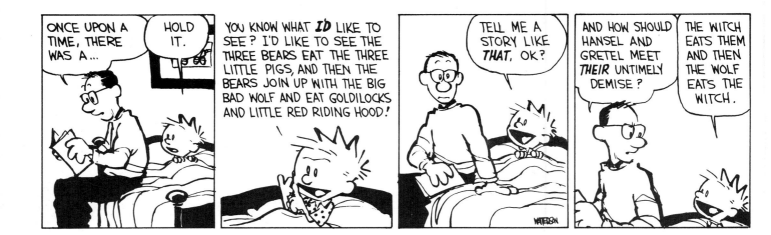

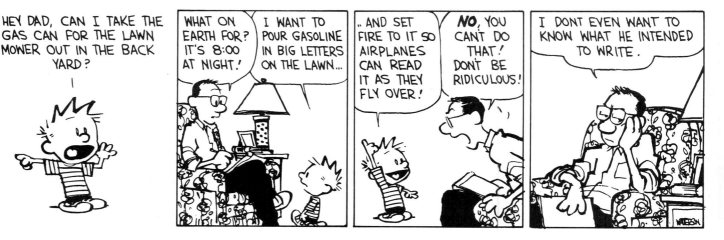

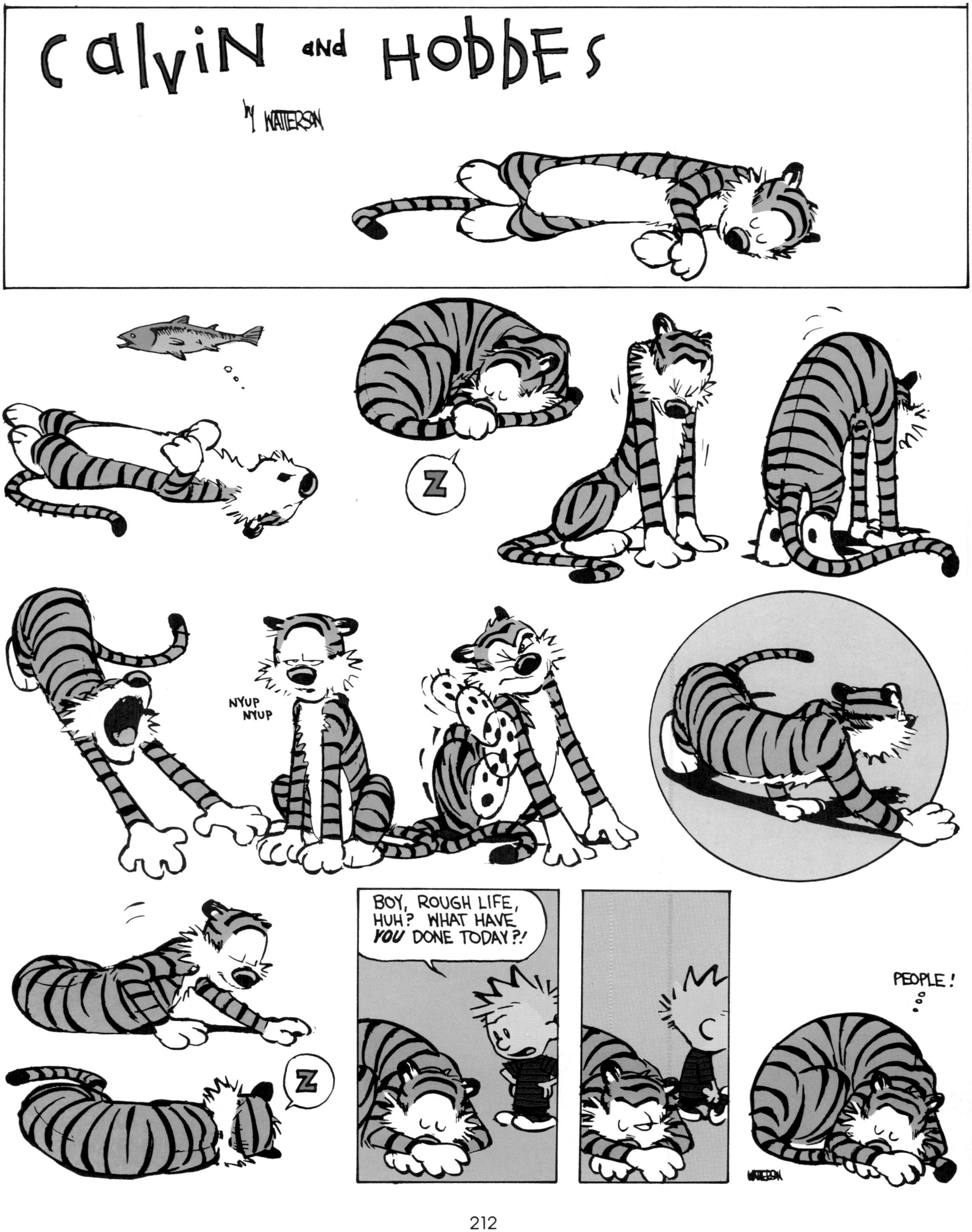
Calvin and HOBBES
by WATTERSON
NYUP NYUP
BOY, ROUGH LIFE, HUH? WHAT HAVE *YOU* DONE TODAY?!
PEOPLE!
WATTERSON

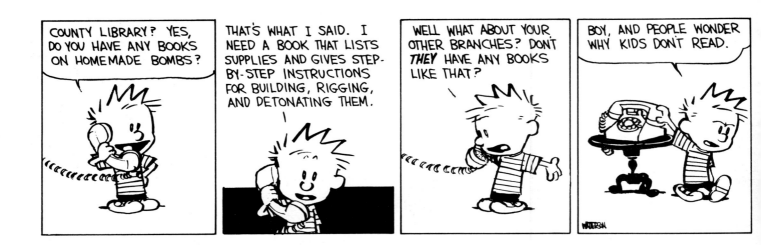

216

218

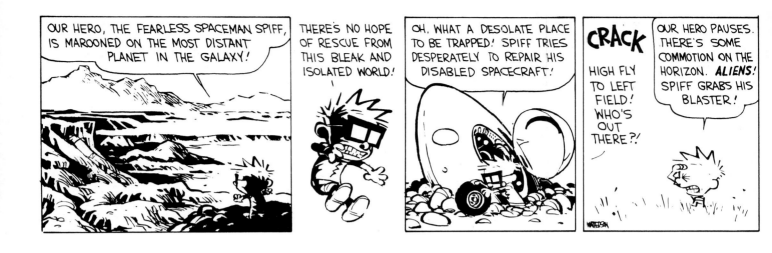

233

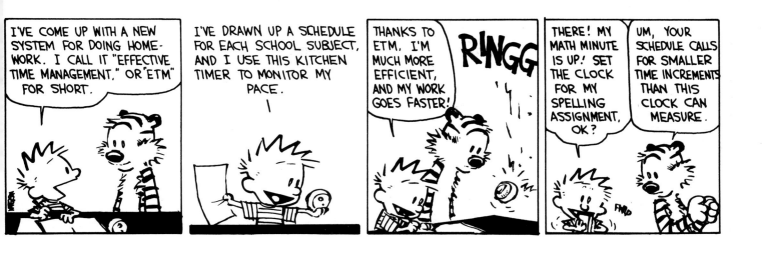

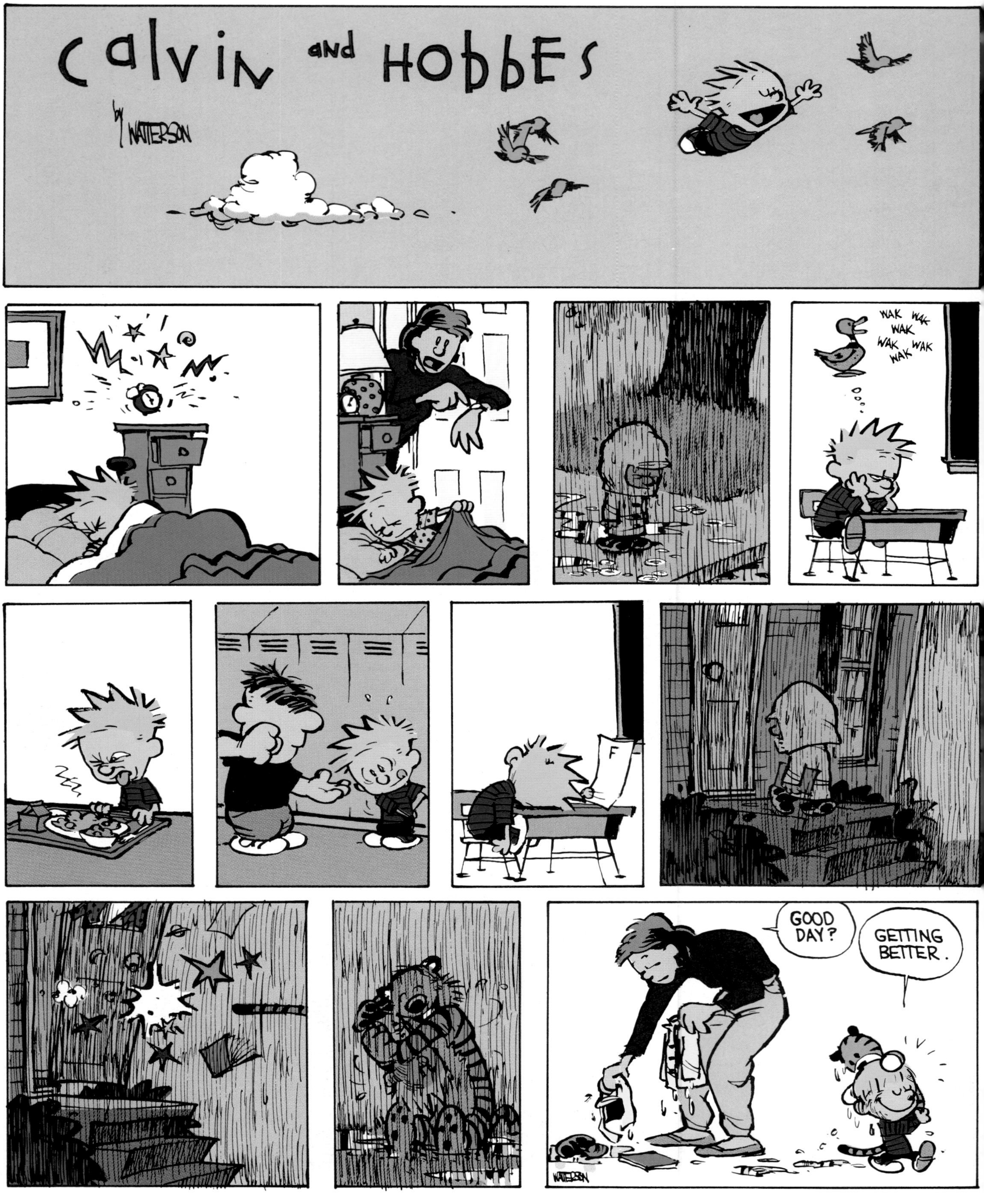
Calvin and HOBBES
by WATTERSON
WAK WAK WAK WAK WAK WAK
F
GOOD DAY?
GETTING BETTER.
WATTERSON

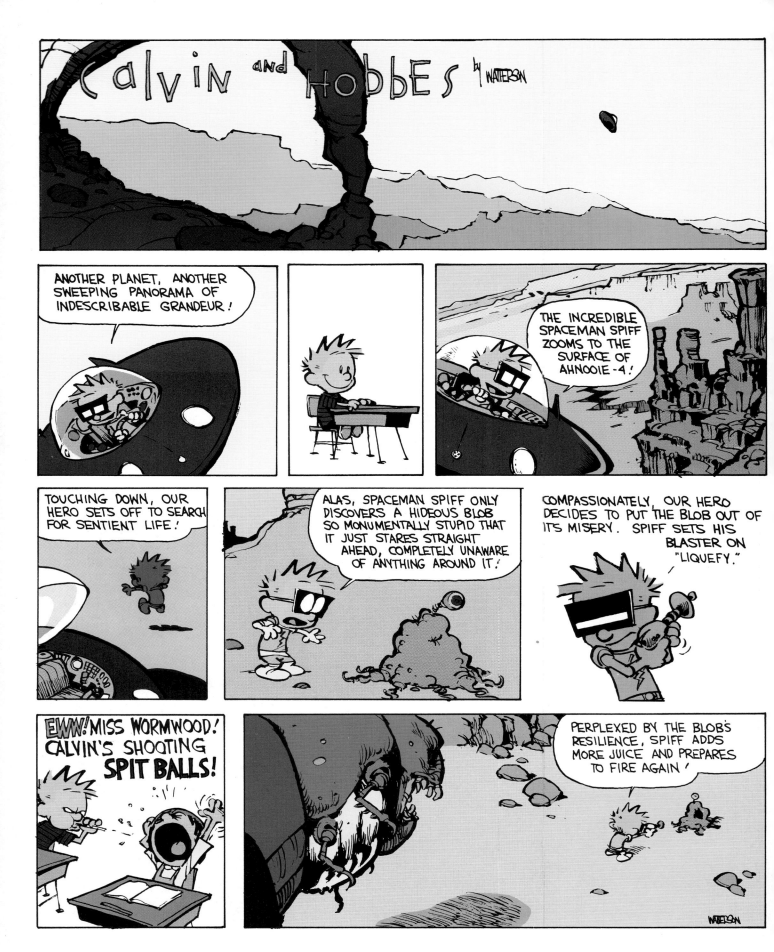

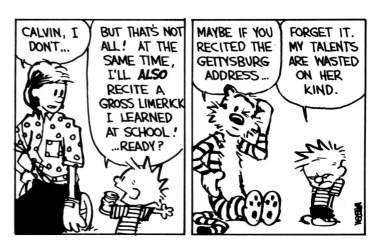

245

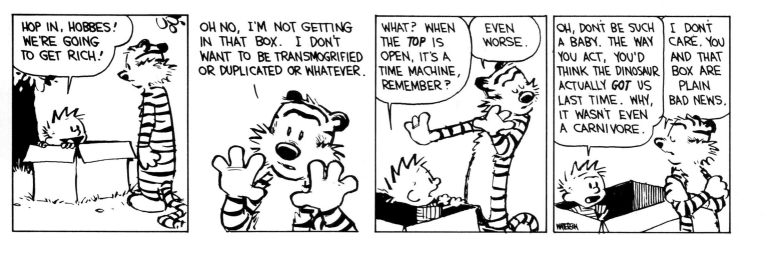

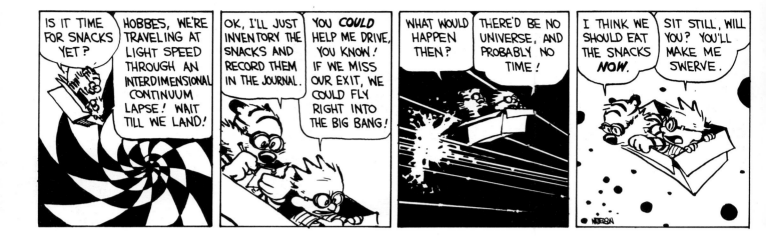

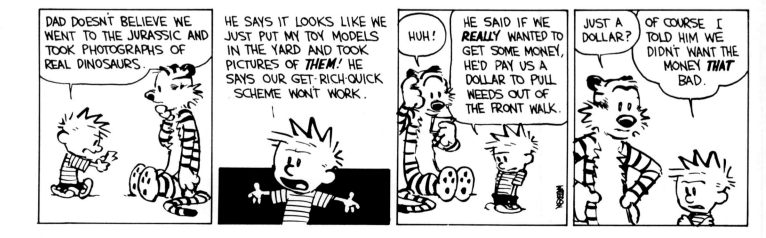

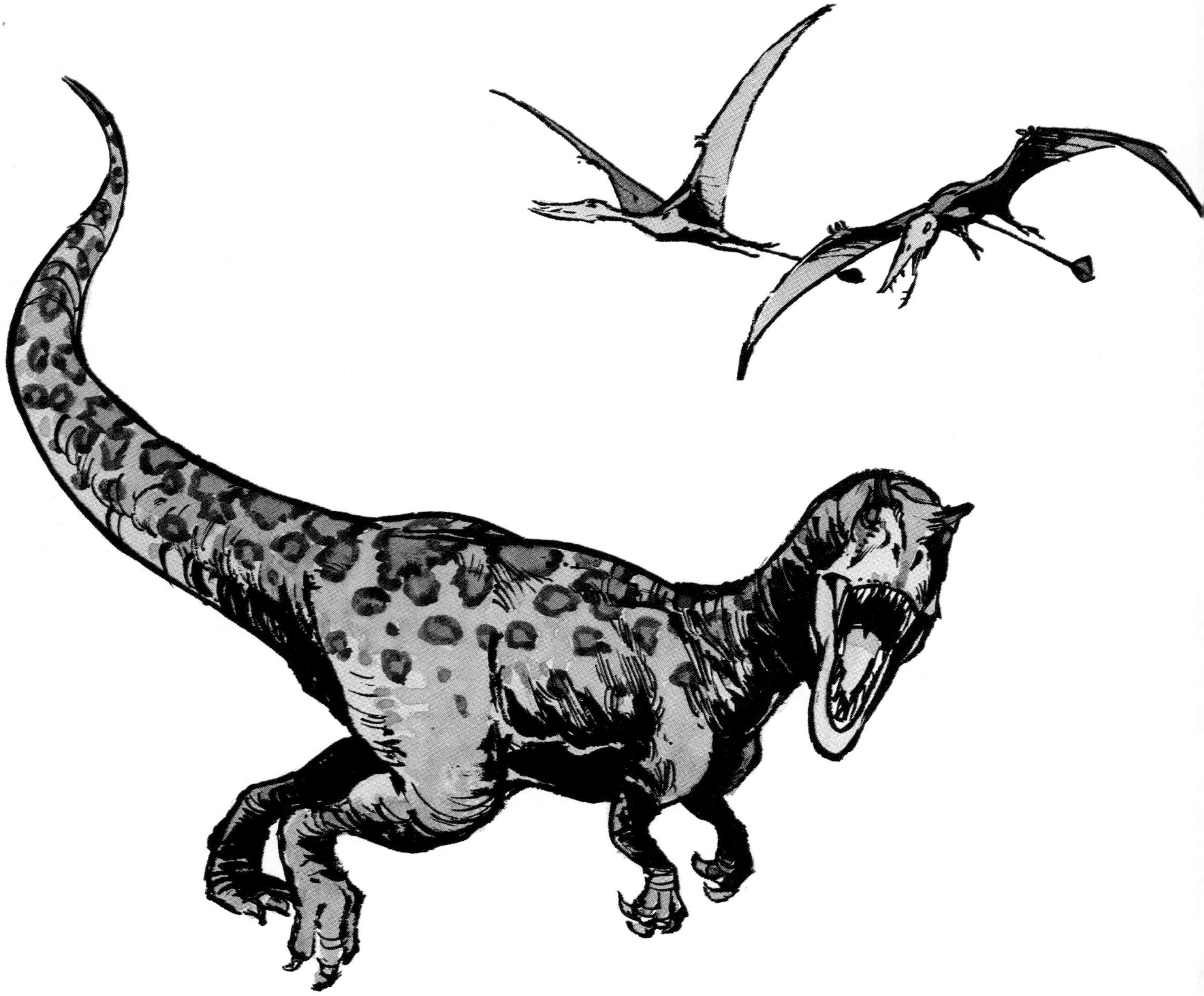

The End